This is a work of fiction, and the views expressed herein are the sole responsibility of the author. Likewise, certain characters, places, and incidents are the product of the author's imagination, and any resemblance to actual persons, living or dead, or actual events or locales, is entirely coincidental.

Wings of our Past
© 2025 Christine Leger

All rights reserved. No part of this book may be scanned, uploaded, reproduced, distributed, or transmitted in any form or by any means whatsoever without written permission from the author, except in the case of brief quotations embodied in critical articles and reviews. Purchase only authorized electronic editions and do not participate in or encourage electronic piracy of copyrighted materials. Thank you for supporting the author's rights.

Published 2025
ISBN: 978-1-0694979-7-0

It was just Grandpa Ron and me today. Mom had to work, and Grandma was away on a business trip. Grandpa said it was a "perfect day to visit the old birds." That's what he calls the planes—especially the ones he used to fix. He always had a twinkle in his eye when he talked about them. I've been to the museum before, but today felt different. Today, Grandpa wasn't just visiting—he was going to tell me all about them.

1

The museum was enormous! Planes of all shapes and sizes hung from the ceiling, stood on the floor, or lined the walls. So many stories waiting to be told.

Grandpa Ron gave my shoulder a squeeze, "Where should we go first, Edmund?"

Grandpa started at the beginning. He pointed to a fragile-looking biplane. "Back then," he said, "we used to build planes out of wood and fabric, like giant kites!" He told me about the Silver Dart, the first powered flight in Canada, and how it only flew a short distance over a frozen lake.

Fact Box: Early Aviation

Canada's first powered flight took place in 1909 with the Silver Dart, piloted by J.A.D. McCurdy. It flew for just over half a mile! Imagine building a plane yourself and then trusting it to fly!

Next, we went to a section about the First World War. Grandpa explained how planes went from being simple observation tools to fierce fighting machines.

He pointed to a Sopwith Camel, its machine guns looking menacing. "Those pilots were incredibly brave," he said. "Flying those flimsy planes in the thick of battle."

Fact Box: The First World War in the Air
Pilots in the First World War faced dangers not only from enemy fire but also from unreliable aircraft. Many planes crashed due to mechanical failures or simply falling apart mid-air! They were true pioneers.

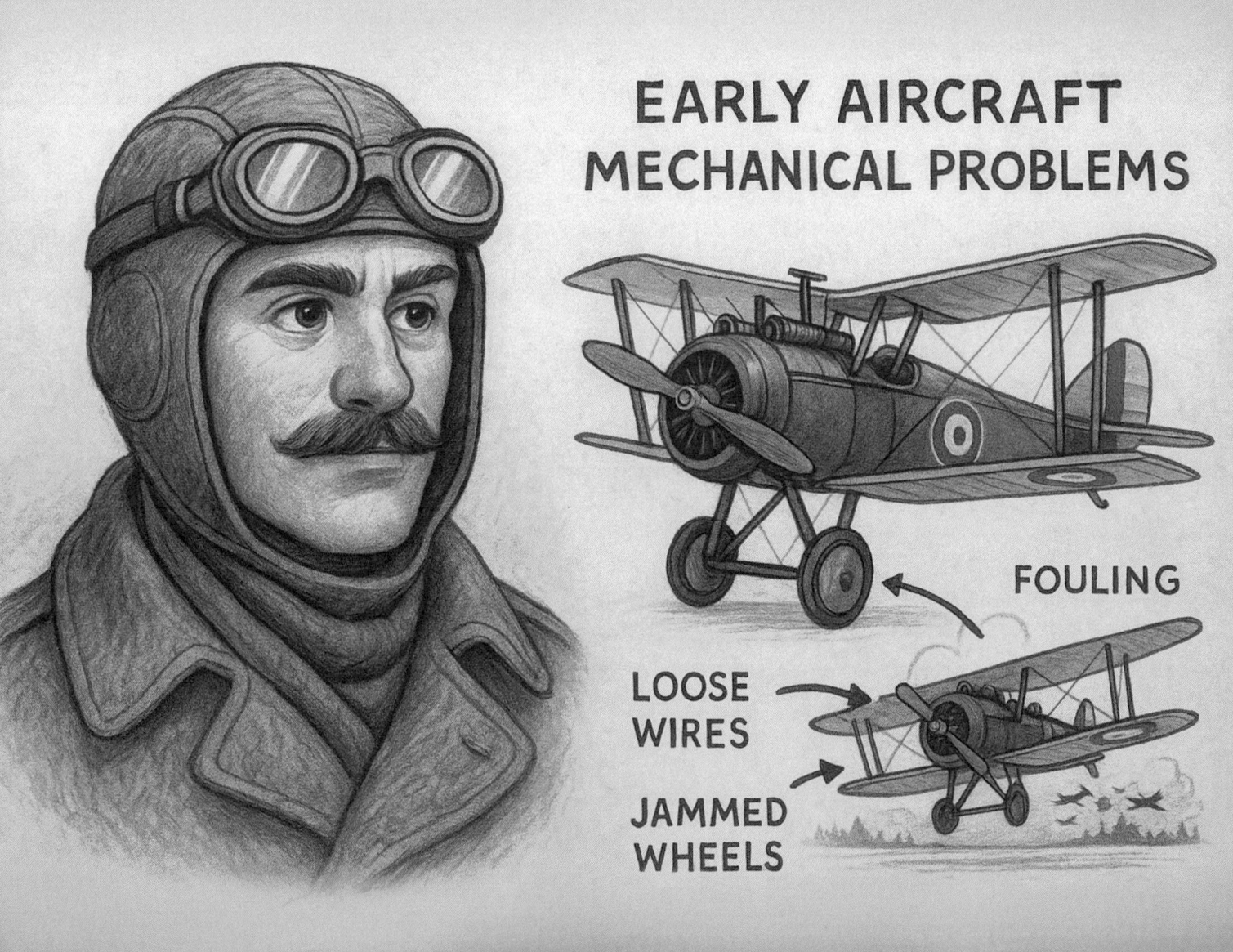

"After the war," Grandpa said, "planes started to open up the North." We walked to a display about bush planes. He told me about pilots who flew mail, medicine, and people to remote communities where there were no roads or railways.

"They were like flying ambulances and post offices all rolled into one!"

Fact Box: Bush Pilots

Bush pilots faced incredible challenges: unpredictable weather, vast distances, and landing on rough, unprepared surfaces like lakes and rivers. They were essential for connecting isolated communities across Canada's vast northern landscape.

The next hall was filled with even bigger and more powerful planes. We saw a Hawker Hurricane, a famous fighter plane from World War II. Grandpa told me how Canadian pilots played a vital role in the Battle of Britain. "They helped defend England from the Nazis," he said.

Fact Box: Canadian Pilots in WWII

Thousands of Canadians served in the Royal Air Force (RAF) during World War II. They flew bombers, fighters, and reconnaissance planes, making a significant contribution to the Allied victory.

PLANES FLOWN BY CANADIANS IN WORLD WAR II

WELLINGTON

HURRICANE

LANCASTER

"After the war came the Cold War," Grandpa explained. "A time of tension between the East and the West." He pointed to a CF-100 Canuck, a jet fighter designed to intercept Soviet bombers. "We had to be ready to defend our skies."

Fact Box: The Cold War in the Air

During the Cold War, Canadian radar stations and fighter jets were constantly on alert, ready to respond to potential threats from the Soviet Union. The DEW Line (Distant Early Warning Line) was a chain of radar stations built across the Arctic to detect incoming bombers.

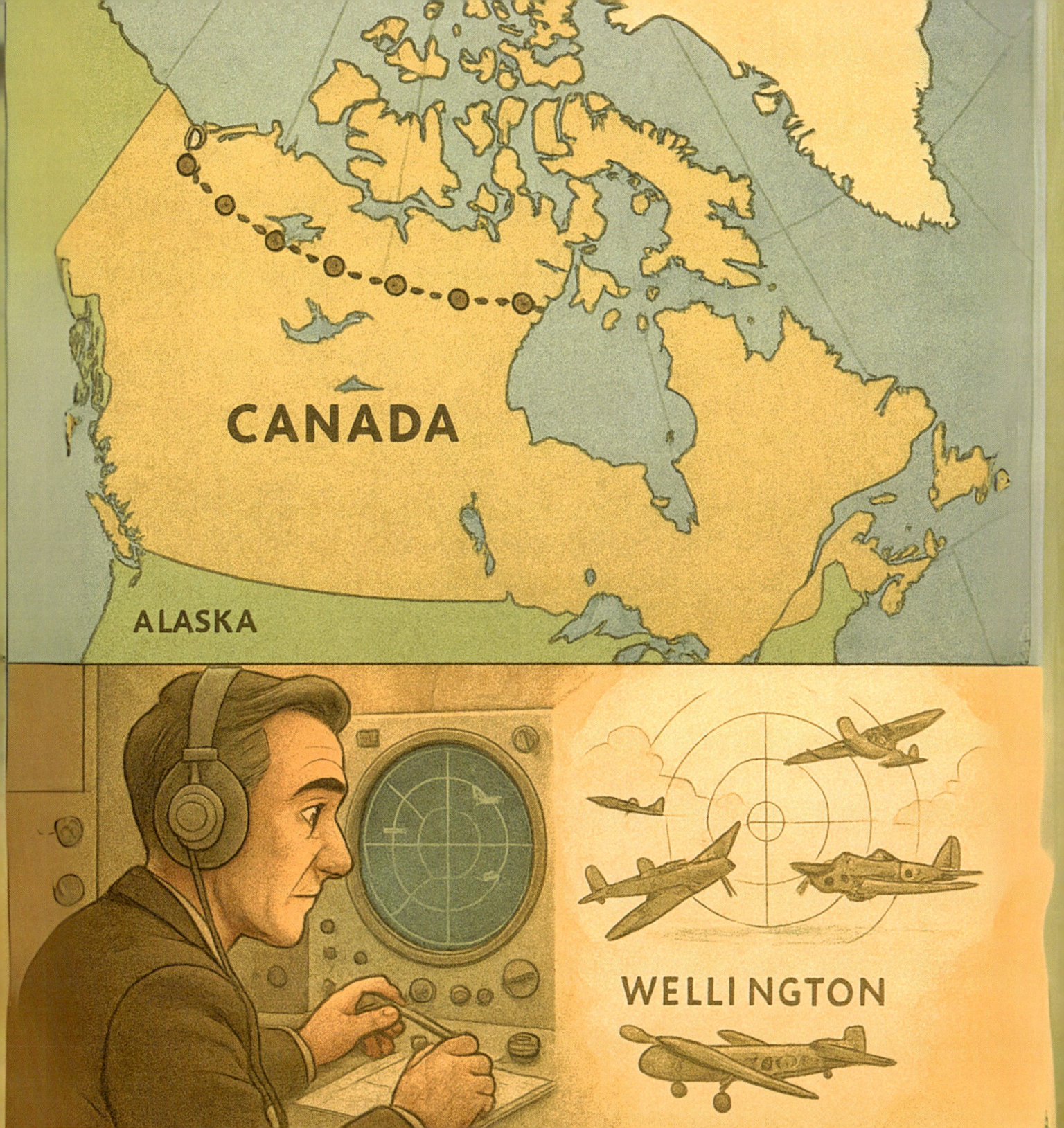

We stood in front of the Hercules. "She's not flashy," Grandpa said. "But she's strong. Reliable. Like a good friend."

He told me how the Hercules flew into ice storms, onto gravel runways, and dropped supplies to places with no roads. "I once spent twelve hours in minus-30 trying to fix her ramp," he chuckled. "Frost in my eyebrows. Worth it."

He pointed to a dent near the tail, "That's from a rogue moose on a runway... she still flew after that!"

Fact Box: The C-130 Hercules

The C-130 Hercules has been used by the Canadian Armed Forces since the 1960s for search and rescue, cargo, and troop transport. It can land on short, icy runways and even dirt strips. It's been all over the world helping people!

We turned the corner, and there she was. The CH-113 Labrador helicopter. Grandpa's eyes softened. "That one saved lives."

He explained how Labradors flew search-and-rescue missions, lowering cable winches into storms to lift people out.

"I wasn't in the sky," Grandpa said, "but I kept her ready to fly." He showed me a photo on his phone of him working on the engine.

Fact Box: The CH-113 Labrador

The Labrador helicopter served Canada from 1963 to 2004. It played a key role in rescuing people during natural disasters, sea accidents, and remote emergencies. Its bright yellow colour made it easy to spot in even the worst weather.

We passed by a large screen, showing the movement of planes across Canada. "Someone has to make sure all these planes don't bump into each other!"

Grandpa explained. He told me about air traffic controllers and the technology they use to keep our skies safe.

Fact Box: Air Traffic Control

Air traffic controllers use radar, radio communication, and complex computer systems to guide planes safely through the sky. They work in control towers and regional centers, managing the flow of air traffic across the country.

We stood before a sleek white model: the Avro Arrow. "She was fast—maybe too fast for her time,"

Grandpa said. He told me about its sudden cancellation, how people still debate it today. "It was a dream that never fully took flight."

Fact Box: The Avro Arrow

The Avro Arrow was a Canadian-made jet interceptor developed in the 1950s. It was ahead of its time but was controversially canceled in 1959. Only a few prototypes were ever built.

Then we walked to the space section. "We didn't just fly," he said. "We reached for the stars."

He showed me a model of the Canadarm, a robotic arm used on the International Space Station. "Canada has always been a part of exploring space."

Fact Box: Canada in Space

Canada has made significant contributions to space exploration with the Canadarm, satellites, and astronauts. Canadian astronauts have flown on the Space Shuttle and the International Space Station, conducting experiments and contributing to our understanding of the universe.

Before we left, Grandpa paused beside a quiet corner. "These machines aren't just metal," he said.

"They're stories. Of people who built, flew, fixed, and dreamed. Stories of courage, innovation, and service."

He turned to me. "And you, Edmund... you're part of that story too. Because you remember."

I smiled. I knew Grandpa was right. The stories of these planes, these pilots, and these builders would live on... in me. I had to write them all down in my notebook.

www.ingramcontent.com/pod-product-compliance
Lightning Source LLC
Chambersburg PA
CBRC090839010526
44119CB00044B/497